Lewis Wilder Hicks

Mr. Ralph Wheelock, Puritan

A paper read before the Connecticut historical society, November 7, 1899

Lewis Wilder Hicks

Mr. Ralph Wheelock, Puritan
A paper read before the Connecticut historical society, November 7, 1899

ISBN/EAN: 9783337084998

Printed in Europe, USA, Canada, Australia, Japan

Cover: Foto ©ninafisch / pixelio.de

More available books at **www.hansebooks.com**

MR. RALPH WHEELOCK
PURITAN

A PAPER READ BEFORE

The Connecticut Historical Society

NOVEMBER 7, 1899

BY

Rev. LEWIS W. HICKS, M. A.

A Member of the Society and a Descendant of Mr. Wheelock

WITH AN APPENDIX
BY
THOMAS S. WHEELOCK

PUBLISHED BY REQUEST

Hartford Press

The Case, Lockwood & Brainard Company

1899

PREFACE

O giving my consent to the publication of the following paper, after its presentation before the Historical Society of Connecticut, I was influenced by a circle of Wheelock friends, to whom I was led to make known its contents several weeks before the public reading. But it seemed to me that the paper should not go out alone, inasmuch as Mr. Thomas S. Wheelock, who has spent much valuable time in tracing out the origin of the Wheelock family, had facts in his possession which cannot but be of special interest to the subscribers for this booklet. I therefore requested him to prepare the subjoined appendix, which will be found to contain important fundamental facts about the lineage and immediate descendants of our common ancestor that will enable present-day descendants, who may so desire, to make independent investigations along the lines of their own particular descent. But in sending out this little production we have had no idea of publishing a " Wheelock Book," in the common acceptation of the term ; nor of making any pecuniary profit out of our conjoint enterprise. Our chief object, (mine in permitting the paper to be published, and Mr. Wheelock's in adding his appendix,) is to lay before the descendants of Mr. Ralph Wheelock some facts about his life and character, which seem never to have been put in a form to give due weight to the influence which our worthy progenitor exerted in the early days of Massachusetts history. In order to insure ourselves against pecuniary loss we have been obliged to charge, what might seem to some, a large price for so small a book. But it should be understood that under the circumstances we could venture to print only a small number of copies, thus increasing the cost of publication, per copy, far beyond what would be involved in the publication of a large edition. For our outlay of time, which has been far from inconsiderable, we ask nothing but the kindly judgment of the kinsmen into whose hands this booklet may come. And it is our hope that some profit and enjoyment may be derived from its perusal by not a few descendants of that grand old Puritan ancestor, whose influence continues to be felt in this land of his adoption, and will be felt so long as Puritan principles and ideals shall continue to exert any power upon the people of our beloved country.

LEWIS WILDER HICKS.

HARTFORD, CONN.

MR. RALPH WHEELOCK
PURITAN

N the brief references to Mr. Ralph Wheelock which are found in biographical
notices of his honored great-grandson,
Dr. Eleazer Wheelock, the first president of Dartmouth College, he is said to have been born in
Shropshire, England, in 1600 A. D., and to have
been educated at Clare Hall, Cambridge. In such
references no allusion is made to his ancestral
antecedents, nor has the most careful examina-
tion of accessible biographical material resulted
in the discovery of his parentage. It is highly
probable, however, that he was a descendant of
Hugh de Whelock who, in the reign of Henry the
Second, received from Roger Mainwaring a title
to all of the latter's claim to the village of Wheelock, in Cheshire County, which he had previously
held. It is also probable that Ralph Wheelock
was a relative of a certain Abraham Wheelock,
who was also a native of Shropshire, who took his
degree of M.A. at Cambridge University in 1618,
was admitted to Clare Hall as a fellow about the

time that Ralph must have entered the same college, and who, later on, became the first professor of the Arabic and Saxon tongues in the university, published, among other important works, an edition of Bede's Ecclesiastical History with the Saxon paraphrase of Alfred, and became the librarian of the university. That Ralph Wheelock was the only one of the Puritan ministers, with whose names we are familiar, to graduate from Clare College (all the others of them, who were Cambridge graduates, taking their degrees from Emmanuel, Jesus, or some other of the several colleges of the university), would seem to point to a special reason for his going to Clare Hall. May that reason not have lain in the fact that he had a scholarly relative there from his own county of Shropshire, the before-mentioned Abraham Wheelock? As the latter was but seven years Ralph's senior, he may have been an elder brother. We shall certainly be pardoned for indulging this supposition ; or at least for holding that Ralph was some sort of a kinsman of the Cambridge professor and librarian. Reasoning backwards from this conjecture we may well believe that our subject was born of " respectable parents," to say the least, and that he was also the child of those who set a high value upon education. Add to what has been said about the family of Wheelock in Cheshire County, to the north of Shropshire, that they had a coat-of-arms, and we are prepared to believe that Ralph Wheelock also belonged to " a family of importance," in the accepted meaning of the expression.

At all events he graduated at Clare Hall in 1626, and took his degree of master of arts there in 1631. Of this college it may be of some interest to know that it was founded in 1326 and bore the name of University College until 1338-9, when, owing to a large gift from Elizabeth Burgh, Countess of Clare, the name was changed to Clare College. The motives which led the noble foundress to endow the institution are so beautifully set forth in her own language that her words are herewith given as follows: " Experience doth plainly teach us, that in every degree, ecclesiastical as well as temporal, skill in learning is no small advantage ; which, although sought for in many ways by many persons, is found in most perfection in the university, where general study is known to flourish. Moreover, when it has been found, it sends out its disciples, who have tasted sweetness, skillful and fit members of God's Church and the state, who shall, as their merits demand, rise to various ranks. . . . We have had in view the object, that the pearl of science . . . may not lie under a bushel but be extended further and wider, and when extended give light to them that walk in the dark paths of ignorance." In a petition addressed in 1445 by Margaret of Anjou to her husband, Henry the Sixth, she speaks of Pembroke College and Clare Hall as being " of grete reputation for good and worshipful clerkis that by grete multitude have be bredde and brought forth in theym." Chaucer, "the father of English Poetry," was reputed to have been a student in Clare Hall; but there is not sufficient proof to warrant the belief that he was ever there in such a capacity. Before the coming of Ralph Wheelock to its quiet cloisters it had sent out a number of scholars who had greatly distinguished themselves in church and state, and its able master during the time of young Wheelock's residence was one of its alumni, Thomas Paske, D.D., by name. As an indication of how the college was regarded at that particular time the following statement may be quoted: " The names of George Ruggle, Nicholas Farrar, Abraham Wheelock, and Augustine Lindsell, among the fellows, are . . . suggestive of an atmosphere of genuine culture." While it is true that a chair of mathematics had not then been established in the University of Cambridge, and Sir Isaac Newton had not been born to give an impetus to scientific investigation; yet Greek, Latin, and Hebrew, and dialectics were thoroughly taught, to the making of close thinkers and sound reasoners. In 1617 the students at the Hall numbered one hundred and ten, which was a little less than the average attendance upon the several colleges which made up the university.

That Ralph Wheelock was a good scholar when he received his master's degree, in 1631, might be presumed from what has already been said. This presumption may be further strengthened when the fact is taken into consideration that John Milton, John Eliot, Samuel Stone, Samuel Eaton, John Norton, Thomas Shepard, and other eminent Puritans were fellow students with him in Cambridge University; and it will be still further confirmed when we shall come to review his career in New England.

That he had been subjected to influences while in the university which had brought him into sympathy with the liberal party of his day, may be inferred from the well-known fact that, as early as the last third of the sixteenth century, Cambridge had become the center of that movement in the national church which gave rise to the use of the name of Puritan; a movement which, from that time on, had become more and more powerful in

2

the university, and which had embraced within its influence many of the choicest of the Cambridge men. This fact, when put with another, that Wheelock was an eminent Puritan minister before he left England, leads to the above conclusion, that when he left Clare Hall with his master's degree he was a Puritan of the Thomas Shepard, Samuel Stone, and George Phillips type, who believed in the reform of the crying abuses of the Church of England, and who would gladly have remained in the mother country to help her work out the problems of church and state which were then confronting her.

It was more than a respectable party to which he joined himself. As the historian, Dr. Palfrey, says: " The Puritanism of the first forty years of the seventeenth century was not tainted with degrading or ungraceful associations of any sort. The rank, the wealth, the chivalry, the genius, the learning, the accomplishments, the social refinements and elegance of the time, were largely represented in its ranks." The same writer says: " The leading emigrants to Massachusetts were of that brotherhood of man who, by force of social consideration, as well as of intelligence and reso-lute patriotism, moulded the public opinion and action of England in the first half of the seven-teenth century." It was with such men that

Ralph Wheelock was identified in England after his graduation; but where he was settled, and what peculiar experiences of a trying nature he endured for conscience' sake, we have had no means of finding out. Sprague, in his "Annals of the American Pulpit," and Drs. McClure and Parish, in their life of Dr. Eleazer Wheelock, speak of him as an eminent non-conformist preacher who suffered persecution for dissenting from the established religion. It is not unlikely that he underwent an experience similar to that of his fellow-student, Thomas Shepard, who says, "he," the bishop, "fired me out of this place," referring to the loss of his living; and who quotes in his autobiography the charge which Laud gave him, as follows: "I charge you that you neither preach, read, marry, bury, or exercise any ministerial functions in any part of my Diocess; for if you do, and I hear of it, I'll be upon your back and follow you wherever you go, in any part of this kingdom, and so everlastingly disenable you." In view of such charges as this, and the accordant treatment to which Laud knew so well how to subject the Puritan clergy, it is no wonder that many of them preferred to brave the dangers of an ocean voyage, to face the rigors of an inhospitable climate, and even expose themselves to the wiles of the Red Men, if so be that they might

worship God after the dictates of their consciences.
If England had no use for them but abuse, they
would go where they could do something for
themselves and their families, and build up a new
commonwealth upon the principles for the establishment of which they had vainly contended in
the mother land. So they came to New England,
no less than sixty graduates of Cambridge and
Oxford coming between the years 1630 and 1639,
the larger part of whom settled in Cambridge,
Massachusetts, and its immediate vicinity. Ralph
Wheelock was one of them. He left England in
1637, (being then in his prime, at the age of thirty-
seven years,) attended by his wife, Rebecca, and
his young child, Gershom. "The ship in which
he embarked was once driven back by tempests,
the voyage was long and distressing," and while
at sea his wife gave birth to a daughter. The
year in which he left old England John Harvard
and John Davenport came to this country; with
the latter of whom, as Dr. Bacon informs us, a
considerable band of colonists came over in the
ship *Hector*. But whether Wheelock was with
either of those Puritan ministers on the voyage
we are not able to affirm. After his arrival he
went to Watertown, that flourishing Puritan
settlement of Massachusetts, from which so many
of our first New England families trace their

descent, but where, in 1637, there were quite
enough families to occupy the farming lands of
the immediate vicinity, and to furnish a surplus
for the colonizing of adjacent territory. Only a
short distance from Watertown, on the other side
of the Charles River, was a beautiful piece of
country, to which some of the Watertown families
had begun to move as early as 1635, and to which
Mr. Wheelock went soon enough after his arrival
in Massachusetts to be reckoned among the early
settlers and one of the efficient founders of what
had become, in 1636, the town of Dedham, but
which was first called "Contentment," a place
that was noted for the generally excellent character of its founders, and that has, up to the present
time, maintained a high standard of citizenship,
culture, and general prosperity. There, with others, Mr. Wheelock was assigned a tract of land,
and began that useful course of life to which
repeated reference was made, at subsequent dates,
in the church and town records of Dedham and
Medfield, but which does not seem to have been
emphasized by any writer to the extent of its
merit. In 1634 a certain William Wood wrote:
" He must have more than a boy's head, and no
less than a man's strength, that intends to live
comfortably. . . . . All New England must
be workers in some kind." That Ralph Wheelock

possessed the necessary qualifications, thus referred to, for comfortable living and for doing useful work in a new country is amply shown in the story which the records tell of his learning, versatility in employment, and success in impressing himself upon the lives of his cotemporaries, and of his own and their descendants.

Now we should naturally look to see this man, who had been trained in the university and who had become eminent as a clergyman, enter upon the work of the minister and follow it as a calling in the new world, as so many of his Puritan associates had done and were doing about him in the vicinity of Boston. But while we are informed that he was asked to take charge of particular churches, and did occasionally preach in settlements about Dedham, yet he did not consent to settle as the pastor of a church, but gave himself up to the doing of such work of a miscellaneous character as might further the material and intellectual, as well as the spiritual, interests of the two new communities with which he successively cast in his lot. It was a saying of Cotton that there was "nothing cheap in New England but milk and ministers." Perhaps it was because others wanted the pulpits, and because his heart was full of the milk of human kindness, that Mr. Wheelock refused to monopolize a pastorate. Be this as it may, without the standing place which the Congregational minister occupied by virtue of his settlement over a church, Ralph Wheelock became a very important factor in the problems which the pioneers had to work out in the early days of Dedham and Medfield. In tracing his services we shall not only follow the course of one man, but shall also be able to form a partial estimate of what was involved in the making of a New England town, as well as of the meaning of the fact that so many of our forefathers were men of high character and of rare cultivation.

The first important thing which Mr. Wheelock is known to have done after moving from Watertown to Dedham was the signing of his name, in July, 1637, to the "Dedham Covenant." His is the tenth name on the list of something over one hundred who, from the time when the first settlers entered the new town until it no longer became obligatory to sign it, subscribed their names to this covenant; which instrument was, in fact, the constitution of that little company of settlers. For it should be remembered that the first code of Colony Laws, known as the "Body of Liberties," was not formed until 1641. This ancient Dedham agreement begins with these beautiful sentences: "We whose names are here unto subscribed, doe in the fear and Reverence

of our Almightie God, Mutually and severally
promise amongst ourselves and each to other to
professe and practice one trueth according to that
most perfect rule, the foundation whereof is
Everlasting Love." The covenant further declares
that all persons were to be excluded from the
Dedham community who were not likely to be
of one heart with the subscribers, and would not
seek with them the good of the whole body rather
than of the individual, to the ends of edification
and peace. Moreover, it provides for a settlement
of differences between disagreeing parties by
reference to two or three persons; imposes the
duty of land-owners to pay their share of taxes
ratably with other men, and announces the purpose of the settlement to be the establishment of
"a loving and comfortable societie." Made up,
as that body of settlers is known to have been, of
exceptionally intelligent men and women, it is
not strange that they should have made some
such provision, that would give promise of assur-
ing to them and to their posterity the continuance
of a well-ordered and moral society. As pioneers
in an enterprise of so much moment, they had a
right to determine the character of the town into
which they were throwing their all. We can
easily believe, then, that to this wholesome covenant Mr. Wheelock signed his name with due

solemnity, and also with joy at the thought of the possibilities which opened before him and his family in a settlement that could only receive those who were like-minded with himself. At all events, the important part which he there played, for something like fourteen years, in connection with the civil, religious, and educational interests of the community, point in this direction. As one of the four persons mentioned in the early records of the town to whose name the prefix of "Mr." was applied, Ralph Wheelock was naturally looked up to, honored in many ways, and enabled to put into effective use the knowledge, abilities, and character which he seems to have possessed to an unusual degree.

As was to have been expected from the character and principles of the thirty or more families that had settled in Dedham up to the year 1637-8, the organization of a church was one of the first things to be considered by them. Indeed, it was for the very purpose of uniting themselves together and worshiping God in churches, after what they believed to be the New Testament order, that they had crossed the sea and planted themselves in the new country. Accordingly, a weekly meeting was established in the year 1637, which was successively held in the several homes of the town, and led in turn by the head of the

3

house where the meeting was appointed. Each
meeting was begun and concluded with prayer,
and some question was taken up and considered
that was of special interest to the body. After
several months had passed in the discussion, at
such meetings, of questions which appertained
to the constitution of a church, to fitness for
church membership, to the proper dispensing of
the ordinances, to duties of brotherly love, and so
on, Mr. John Allin, a graduate of Cambridge (who
had settled in Dedham in 1637, at the invitation
of the entire body of citizens, with a view to his
looking after their spiritual interests), set about
the work of organizing the much-talked-of church.
In the history which he wrote of the beginnings
of the First Church in Dedham, he informs us
that his first act was to commit the case to Mr.
Wheelock, that he might obtain his assistance in
determining whether the Lord, upon opening up
their spiritual conditions, would so far unite their
hearts that they two should agree upon a third
person as being worthy to enter into fellowship
with them, with a view to the three agreeing upon
a fourth, and so on, until a sufficient number might
be found to organize the desired church.   Of the
difficulty which those two Cambridge graduates
had in finding eight persons in that select body of
good people whom they could conscientiously ac-

cept as being in every respect worthy to be the nucleus of a church, of the grounds of objection which they and the first four of the elect felt obliged to interpose to the immediate acceptance of others; and of the preliminary steps, such as heart-searchings, fastings, and special meetings for prayer, which finally led up, in September, 1638, to the actual formation of a church of eight members,— of all these things time would fail in the telling, although the story, as penned by Mr. Allin, is a most interesting one, and might possibly suggest some wholesome lessons to church organizers in this hurrying period of the world's history. Neither is there space to dwell upon the setting apart of John Hunting to the eldership, nor to the ordination of John Allin, and his installation as the first pastor of that carefully chosen body of Puritan saints.   It is enough for the purpose of this paper that throughout all of those momentous proceedings Ralph Wheelock was the right hand man of Mr. Allin, and that he bore a conspicuous part, by the laying on of his hands, in the ordination services, which gave to the new ecclesiastical organization the two chief officers which the good people of Dedham believed to be necessary for the official equipment of a true church of Christ.   Laboring in perfect agreement with his fellow alumnus of old Cambridge, al-

though Mr. Allin, and not himself, was the choice
of the people for the honorable office which he
was helping to fill; acting, too, in the interest of
the purity of the church, as against the admission
of some who, as we may well believe, may have
been tempted to take offense at his action against
them; and also maintaining, during all those
months of anxiety, a prayerful and serene spirit,
which qualified him for the solemn duties which
he was appointed to discharge in the ordination
services, Mr. Wheelock commends himself to us
as a man of strong character, of deep religious
feeling, of pleasing tactfulness, and hence as one
to whom his fellow citizens would naturally have
turned to fill their places of trust and responsi-
bility. And the Dedham records show us that
they did turn to him and repose the largest confidence in his character and judgment. A record
under the date of December, 1639, reads as follows: "Whereas ye wholl towne weare warned
to meete together this Daye to make choyce of
neue men for ye ordering of the Towne affayers
according unto a Courte Order in that behalf,
The greatest pte of ye Inhabiting townsmen
being assembled accordingly made choyce as Fol-
loweth, viz. Mr. Raffe Whelocke, John Kings-
bury, John Luson, John Bacheler, John Haward,
Eleazer Lusher, John Dwite, Robert Hinsdell."

At that meeting it was also voted that whatever power the whole town had, when acting together, should be put into the hands of these eight persons, for the term of one year; which act was certainly an indication of the confidence which the town had in their first selectman. In addition to the duties which this appointment required to be performed in conjunction with his seven associates, and they could have been neither few nor small in the development of that new community, Ralph Wheelock had other duties laid upon him, from time to time, for which his collegiate training had well fitted him. For instance, he was appointed to assist the measurer in laying out the town; in 1642 was appointed by the General Court clerk of writs and one of the commissioners to end small causes in Dedham; and in 1645 was authorized to solemnize marriages, which pleasant privilege at that time, as will be remembered, was one that belonged to the civil officer rather than to the minister of the gospel. He was also deputed, with two others, "to make a rate for charges about ye meting house and other charges annexed thereunto." When we take all these duties into consideration, and remember that Mr. Wheelock was a land owner, and was probably dependent for his living, to a large extent at least, upon the products of his estate, we must conclude that those first years of his life in the settlement at Dedham must have been very busy ones, as well as greatly serviceable to his fellow townsmen.

But we have now only reached that point in his life where his influence began to be felt to a degree that has proved itself to have been of a most impressive and far-reaching nature ; a point which was not only important in his life, but which must also be conceded to have marked the beginning of a new order of things in Massachusetts history, if not in a still wider field. The point of time referred to was the first day of February, 1644. On that memorable day forty-one males of Dedham met together in town meeting and took the following recorded action : " The Inhabitants taking into Consideration the great necessitie of providing some means for the Education of the youth of sd Towne did with an unanimous consent declare by voate their willingness to promote that worke promising to put too their hands to provide maintenance for a Free School in our said Towne, and farther resolve and consent testifying it by voate to rayse the sume of Twenty pounds ℔ annu ; towards the maintaining of a schoole Mr to keep a free school in our sd Towne. And also did resolve and consent to betrust the sd 20£ per annu & certaine lands in sd

Towne, formerly set apart for publique use, into the hand of the feofees, to be presently chosen by themselves, to imploy the sd 20£ and the land afores'd, to be improved for the use of said schoole: that as the profits shall arise from the said land, every man may be proportionally abated of his some of the sd 20£ aforesaid. And that the said feofees shall have the power to make a rate for the necessary charge of improving the said land, they giving account thereof to the Towne, or to those whom they should depute." The school which, in accordance with the foregoing enactments, was established in Dedham, in 1644, is declared on good authority to have been the very first free school supported by a town tax that was opened in Massachusetts. It is true that the Massachusetts law of 1642 required that schools should be established in every town. But it left them to be sustained by tuition fees, or in such other ways as the towns might choose. The first enactment of that State "charging that each municipality" should "have a schoolmaster set up" was passed in 1662, and fifteen years later was made obligatory on all places of fifty families. Plymouth's school, which was started in 1672, is claimed to have been the first free school that was *established by law*. Dorchester, indeed, had appropriated, as early as

1639, the rentage of Thomson's Island, which had been granted the town by the General Court several years before for the maintenance of a school. But notwithstanding all this, what has been before asserted is doubtless true, that in their enactments of 1644, whereby the sum of 20£ and the profits of certain public lands were appropriated by vote for the support of a free school, the freemen of Dedham did inaugurate in Massachusetts a new system for the education of her children, a system the wisdom of which has been demonstrated by the more than two hundred and fifty years of her experience along the general lines which were marked out by those forty-one Puritan settlers of Dedham. The surnames of some of those two score and one pioneers have come down to us in very distinguished associations. Our Ralph Wheelock was at that memorable town meeting, and he was the ancestor of the first two presidents of Dartmouth College. John Dwight was there, and he was the ancestor of the two Timothy Dwights, so well known as the able presidents of Yale College. Richard Evered was one of the forty-one attendants at the meeting, and he was the ancestor of President Edward Everett, of Harvard College. Anthony Fisher was also there, and he was the ancestor of the renowned statesman and friend of Washington, Fisher Ames, who declined the presidency of Harvard College in 1804, after he had been elected to that office. And the ancestor of the two governors Fairbanks, of Vermont, was present, to give his vote in favor of the free school. A notable company that truly was, if what they did at the meeting and the honor which has been reflected back upon them by a distinguished posterity be taken into consideration. Surely their names, as well as their act, are worthy of being handed down to the remotest generations, and to be forever associated with the beneficent free school system, under which our country has made such remarkable progress in everything that makes for the enlightenment of a free people.

But the establishment of that free school in Dedham has an additional interest for those who care to perpetuate the memory of Mr. Wheelock; for the tradition has come down to us that he was the first teacher of that now famous school. The tradition, moreover, is so well supported by two or three facts of a confirmative nature that we have no good reason for doubting that from 1644 until 1651, the date of his leaving Dedham, he did instruct the children of that goodly town in the school which his wisdom had helped to establish. The facts referred to are these: that during the seven years between 1644 and 1651 Mr. Whee-

4

lock's name is not associated in the records with other important matters, as it had been during the previous years; that we have the definite statement in the record of Dec. 12, 1648, that when the selectmen of the town were considering the plan of a schoolhouse, his "motion for advice was answered," as if he, the schoolmaster, were taking an important part in the furtherance of the projected enterprise of erecting a new school building; and that he is certainly known to have taught school afterwards in the new town of Medfield. These three facts would seem to amply support the tradition, and therefore to justify the belief that Ralph Wheelock taught the first free school in Massachusetts, and one of the first in New England, that was supported directly by a town tax. In cherishing this belief posterity may well assign him the added honor of having been the teacher of certain ancestors of a most remarkable group of teachers, and hence the possible, to say the least, the possible source of an hereditary bias, which worked itself out in pedagogic lines in succeeding generations, to a wonderful extent. If it was the case, as doubtless it was, that Mr. Wheelock taught his own son, Eleazer, with the rest of the children there in Dedham, and taught young Timothy, the son of John Dwight, who was then of the right age to

attend school, and also taught the son of Richard
Evered, from whom Edward Everett was descended; then he had in his school the ancestors
of at least five college presidents who have made
their impress upon three of our New England colleges, and hence upon thousands of the bright
young men of our beloved land. The fact that a
bias towards the teaching function actually had
its beginning in him, which was propagated in
four of his own descendants, of two or three following generations, who were teachers of more or
less note, argues strongly in favor of the supposition before stated, that, through his peculiar fitness for the work which was laid upon him in
Dedham, he did set in motion a wide current of
pedagogic influence which afterwards worked itself into the admirable instruction of the five college presidents whose names add luster to the
reputation of three of our New England colleges.
However this may have been, there seems to be
no ground for doubting the wisdom of his choice
of the profession of a teacher, instead of following that calling which was so overcrowded when
he came to Massachusetts. And just here, in the
consciousness which he may have had of his sin-
gular fitness for the work of the teacher, may perhaps be seen the determining cause for his refus-
ing to accept the offer of pastorates when he was

called to them. He was a born teacher, and a
teacher of youth he would be whenever the op-
portunity came to him.

We have already seen how important was the
part which Mr. Wheelock took in the affairs of
Dedham during the earlier years of its history.
We now turn to another chapter of his life, which
we find in connection with the formation of a
new town. As early as the year 1649 the inhabitants of Dedham began to consider the matter of
making a new township out of a part of their
superabundant territory, which then embraced
what are now known as the towns of Dedham,
Norwood, Walpole, Norfolk, Wrentham, Franklin,
Bellingham, Medfield, Dover, Needham, Welles-
ley, and parts of Natick and Hyde Park. As it
was then necessary for the residents of a place
to have their houses grouped together in order to
secure protection from the depredations of the
Indians, there was only one way in which a town
could make any general use of its outlying landed
possessions, and that was the forming, or sanc-
tioning the formation, of colonies, and sending
them out to occupy a portion of its virgin soil.
And this is precisely what the town of Dedham
did, with Ralph Wheelock as the leader of the
first movement in this direction. In November,
1649, to him and six others was committed by the

freemen of Dedham the duty of "erecting, disposing, and government of" a new village until there was such a company of men engaged in that plantation and associated together as the town of Dedham judged "meet for that work and trust." This body of seven men acted in behalf of the parent town for fifteen months, until May, 1651, when the new town of Medfield was granted the usual full powers of an independent town by the General Court of Massachusetts. Three of the seven, Mr. Wheelock, Thomas Wight, and Robert Hinsdale, left Dedham with the colonists, but the others, John Dwight among them, remained in the mother settlement. As it had been at the laying of the foundations of Dedham, so it now was at Medfield,— an instrument was drawn up for all to sign who desired to be accepted as inhabitants of the colony. This instrument was called "An Agreement," concerning which Tilden, the historian of Medfield, says: "Its author is not certainly known; but there is little doubt that it was chiefly, if not entirely, the work of Ralph Wheelock, who has very properly been styled 'the founder of Medfield.'" The agreement is too long to be incorporated entire in this paper, but the last two of the three "resolves" which follow the preamble are of sufficient interest to merit our attention, since they are indicative of the spirit of the man who prepared them, as well as of the temper of the colonists who affixed their names to the instrument. The following are the second and third resolves: "That if differences, questions, or contentions shall fall out, or arise, any manner of ways in our societie, or betwixt any parties therein, that they shall really endeavor to resolve and issue the same in the most peaceable ways & manner, by refference, Arbitration, or some other the like means before it shall com to any place of publicke Judicature, except it be in our own Towne. That we shall all of us in the said Towne faithfully endeavor that only such be receaved to our societie & Township as we may have sufficient satisfaction in, that they ar honest, peaceable, & free from scandal and erroneous opinnions." Thus was every possible precaution taken to secure for the new town only such settlers as would be willing to labor for the welfare and good name of the community; a precaution which did actually result in gathering together a choice body of inhabitants, and in the formation of another settlement of the Dedham type, which was the forty-third town in the colony in the order of incorporation. Within a very few months after the incorporation of the town, Mr. John Wilson, a graduate of Harvard College, and a son-in-law of Rev. Thomas Hooker of Hartford, commenced his labors in Medfield as pastor of its church, Mr. Wheelock probably thinking that he could be of greater service to the community in the performance of other duties than those which appertained to the calling of the minister. During the first four years of Medfield's history, and for a single year at a subsequent period, he was one of the town's selectmen. He was made a magistrate, was commissioned to perform the marriage ceremony, and, in 1656, married the first pair who were united in Medfield. In 1653 he was chosen to take up a collection for Harvard College, to which institution, more than twenty years later, he, with threescore others, is credited with having made another contribution. He was also sent by his fellow-townsmen to Boston, for the years 1663, '64, '66, and '67, as a deputy to the Great and General Court, thus rounding out his service to the town in a way which bore testimony to the high esteem in which he was held by the community at large. That he was called upon to represent Medfield during those four particular years, when the Massachusetts Bay Colony was greatly disturbed over the effort which Charles the Second was making to limit its independence, would seem to clearly point to the special confidence which his fellow-citizens had in his wisdom as a councilor. But it seems to have been his chief business in Medfield, as it had been for seven years in Dedham, to give instruction to the young. In 1655 the town voted £15 to establish "a schoule for the education of the children, to be raised by a rate according as men have taken up lands, and the rest of the maintainance to be raised upon the children that goe to schoule." Of this school it is known that Mr. Wheelock was the master, but just how long he presided over it we are unable to say. From the following record of 1668: "Mr. Wheelock was employed to keep a school for such of the youth as should come to him to learn to read and write, for the salary of ten shillings a week," it is supposable that he taught the school from the time of its institution until he became a representative to the General Court, a period of eight years, and that, after he had concluded his labors in the legislature, he was authorized by the above town vote to resume the work for which he had shown such exceptional fitness, although he was then about sixty-eight years old. And it is not improbable, in view of the statement of McClure and Parish, that "the residue of his life he passed in various useful labors, and principally in the instruction of youth," that he actually spent the fifteen remaining years of his life in teaching the young of Medfield out of his stores

of knowledge and experience. At all events, the
picture of the aged man gathering the children
about him and giving them instruction until he
himself was called upon to become a learner in
the higher school above, is a pleasing one; and it
certainly falls in with the statement made concerning him, that "he lived to a good old age,
universally beloved and respected, and deceased
Nov., 1683, in the 84th year of his age."

Now there are many things that we should be
glad to know about this Puritan minister, schoolmaster, and citizen, concerning which we know
little or nothing. For instance, we should be
pleased to know whether he was short or tall, fat
or lean, blue-eyed or black-eyed, slow of speech or
impassioned in his delivery of sermon, teaching,
and address; and all the other characteristics
which together made up his personality, helped
determine the course of his life and made him,
what he certainly was, eminently useful to his
own generation, and an influence to impress succeeding generations for good. Moreover, it
would greatly interest his posterity to know more
about his wife than the facts that her name was
Rebecca and that she had to affix her mark,
instead of her name, to the documents which she
signed; although such illiteracy in a woman was
the common thing in those days, rather than the

exception ; not a few educated men holding, as did John Milton, that their daughters were better off without an education. And we should be pleased to know more about Mr. Wheelock's nine children, concerning whom we have some good reasons for believing that they were in general a credit to their estimable parents. It would also gratify our curiosity to know why it was that this schoolmaster's estate, which was rated at £274 10s. in 1652, soon after his removal from Dedham to Medfield, was only worth £190 in 1660. Did teaching school in those early New England days impoverish a man, as it has been known to do in more recent times? Or did Mr. Wheelock's known interest in the cause of education lead the financial agents of Harvard College to make annual visits to Medfield, to solicit funds for that worthy institution ? Or was it the case that other claimants upon his sympathies also drew so heavily upon his resources that his property shrank about one-third in eight years, and he was therefore impelled to leave his favorite occupation for four years, to eke out his slender income through the salary of a legislator ? But we shall probably have to wait for the satisfaction of such pardonable curiosity until that future when we may be permitted to see the faces, and hear the voices of those whom we have only known through the voice of tradition and the limited introduction of the printed page.

However, there are certain things of a very positive nature that grow out of a study of such lives as the one that has been partially set forth in this sketch, some of which it may not be unprofitable to emphasize as we bring our paper to its conclusion. The first of them is this, that we can never be too grateful to Almighty God that in His plans for the settlement of this part of America "He sifted a whole nation, that He might send choice grain over into this wilderness," as William Stoughton put it in 1669. We can never be adequately thankful for the providence which turned the tide of Puritan emigration towards our New England shores, rather than towards some other land, or even towards some other part of our own land where the Puritan character would have had a less favorable field for its manifestation, and for the solving of the vital problems which it so nobly wrought out for the benefit of posterity. After all due credit has been given to the Pilgrims for the heroic work which they accomplished on the bleak shores of Massachusetts, it must not be forgotten that it was "the *Arbella* with its Puritan cargo, and not the *Mayflower* that brought to Massachusetts Bay the royal charter, which," as some one has said, " gave the guaranties of local self-government, and which may be said to have foreshadowed the future independence of the people of Massachusetts." Yes, and we should remember that it was other ships which, later on, brought over Puritans like John Harvard, Thomas Shepard, and Ralph Wheelock, to give an impetus to the development of sound learning in Massachusetts; and Thomas Hooker, John Haynes, Samuel Stone, John Davenport, and the Eatons, to lay splendid foundations for educational and civic institutions in Connecticut; and a host of other intelligent and able Puritans to do the like for other parts of our dear New England. For such providential guidance the entire nation has abundant reason for cherishing a spirit of gratitude towards Him, by whom, as we are taught, the destinies of all nations are directed.

Of another thing we may be well assured, that we cannot cherish too loyally and lovingly the memory of the noble men who braved the dangers which were incident to the pioneer work that they had to do in this new land, thousands of miles distant from dear old England. Refined, as they were, and fitted to enjoy all the high privileges to which their birth and position entitled them, and unused to the deprivations and the hard labors which their new life necessitated, their heroic bearing — sublime courage, patience, perseverance, and industry — cannot but challenge our admiration and win the highest regard for their memories.

" Here were men (co-equal with their fate)
  Who did great things, unconscious they were great."

Not to perpetuate their deeds and embalm their memories in biographic, historic, narrative, and poetic literature; and in bronze, marble, and granite, would lay upon their posterity the charge of having been unfaithful to their ancestral benefactors; for benefactors those noble Puritans were of all who have inherited their names and have entered into the enjoyment of the privileges which, by sacrifice, they secured for unborn millions.

And one thing more we know right well, that it belongs to those who are justly proud of what the Pilgrim and Puritan fathers did to carry on the work which they came across the sea to do, until it shall have been completed; until liberty to worship according to the dictates of the conscience, civil freedom, free education, and representative government shall have been given to all men over whom our nation has secured any power. To refuse to do, at the cost of comparatively small sacrifice, what the fathers did through the greatest sacrifices, would prove that

we have not truly cherished the fathers' memories, and that we have degenerated from the high
ideals which they set before themselves, and
which, in their heroic efforts, they measurably
reached. We can best honor them as, with faith
in their God, and faith in ourselves as the appointed successors of those early New England
worthies, we build solid institutions for the
people, both religious and civic, wherever we
may, whether in America, on the islands of the
sea, or on other continents where our high
privileges have never been enjoyed. If a study
of such lives as that of Ralph Wheelock and of
his Puritan associates teaches us anything that
is of real value it certainly teaches this with an
irresistible emphasis. Hence the American people might well adopt as their own the language of
a modern poet, and say from the heart : —

> " Our fathers tamed the wilderness
>   And wrested from the sullen earth
>   Its largess, and with power and worth
>   And full faith in the future wrought
>   With might of deed and might of thought.
>   No sluggards they, with craven fears ;
>   They faced with high, undaunted hearts
>   The stern front of the coming years.
>
>   .   .   .   .
>
> " We will not shame our history,
>   We will not falter on the road

Appointed by the Most High God ;
'Twas He who held us by the hand,
And led us to the light of day —
'Twas he who made our eyes to see,
And oped our minds to understand
The blessed creed of liberty.

" We may not pause, we may not wait
And lie beside the sheaf and vine
Content with sordid bread and wine.
We have but climbed the lower slope,
And far above us and beyond
The summits tower in the sky
Whence we may view the glorious scope,
And prospect of our destiny."

LEWIS WILDER HICKS.

APPENDIX.

HE foregoing address by the Rev. Lewis W. Hicks, which so ably portrays the noble character of our ancestor, and which so clearly and satisfactorily shows the beneficence of Ralph Wheelock's influence as an educator of youth and counselor in religious and public affairs (the rich fruitage of which has been descending to succeeding generations), has led to the suggestion that Mr. Hicks's facts might well be supplemented by other matters relative to the Wheelock family that could not appropriately appear in the address before the Historical Society, but might be included in this publication, as an appendix. Of the writer, who has made some research in the records which touch upon the life of the Wheelocks, both in Old England and New England, a request was made that he should contribute, in some measure, such matter as might prove interesting to living descendants of Ralph Wheelock. Accordingly, the following is cheerfully contributed to this end.

The genealogy of Ralph Wheelock is obscure.

Apparently no successful effort has been made to trace it. That he came from Shropshire County, England, a county lying just south of Cheshire county, in which there is still a town, or parish, known as " Wheelock," is certain. To that part of England we should therefore naturally look for the origin of the family. In "Ormerod's History of Cheshire" the name of "Whelok" appears as of the time and reign of Henry II, about the year 1200 A. D. The book records the name as " de Quelok," " de Whelok," and " Wheelock," and recites that " Roger Mainwaring released to Hugh de Whelok all his claim to the village of Whelok, which he (the said Hugh) held of Richard de Moston his knight ; " and "not long after, Adam de Whelok gave to his brother Hugh all his right to this place — and 1285, Thomas de Whelok bought the lands of Randle, son of Nicolas de Blackwood." "Thomas de Whelok of Whelok had letters of exemption from service on juries, perhaps for military services; and same year, had Letters of Protection on his departure for Ireland in the train of Robert de Vere, duke of Ireland." Wm. Venables of Kinderton brought two writs against Adam, son of Adam de Bostock and others, for taking away the body of Richard, son of John, son of Thomas de Whelok, and the custody of 16 mess. &c. (1 mill, and 452 acres),

which John held of him by knight's service, ever
since which time the Wheloks were under lords
hereof, till Thomas, son of Richard de Whelok
died s. p. 1439, at which time Agnes, wife of
Richard de Leversage, but daughter to Elizabeth,
sister to John, father of Richard de Whelok
above mentioned, was found the cousin and next
heir." Ormerod further recites that "the son of
this Thomas de Quelok, viz. Thomas de Quelok,
occurs as one of the lessees of the town of Middle-
wich, as Thomas de Quelok purveyor to the King
in the hundred of Northwich in a recog. in 100s
to bring " to Chester within a certain day, all the
corn and bacon charged upon the said Hundred,'"
etc. Furthermore, it is stated that "Thomas de
Whelok and Julian his wife, then obtained from
Ralph de Hassale, chaplain, the manor of Whelok
for life; remainder to Thomas his son and Alice
his wife, and their heirs forever." The name of
Thomas again occurs as one who had been appointed collector of a subsidy; and still again as
lord of Whelok Manor. The village or Manor of
Whelok appears to have passed into possession of
the Leversage family about 1438-9. The Wheelocks who thus early became extinct, as a family,
in the township which was called by their name,
were probably survived by lines of yeomanry
bearing the same name, who were settled in Bec-

ton and Hassall, where the parent house held lands; and later on were widely scattered through the counties of Cheshire, Shropshire, and elsewhere. And there can be no reasonable ground for doubting that it was from some one of the descendants of the Hugh de Whelok, mentioned above, that Ralph Wheelock was descended. Indeed, it is the opinion of the writer that his ancestry could readily be traced to the Wheelocks of "Wheelock," Cheshire County, by reference to the records of Becton and Hassall, England,— records which are not obtainable in this country; and it is the opinion of Mr. Hicks that the records of Whitchurch, in northern Shropshire, the birthplace of Abraham Wheelock, would throw still further light upon his later ancestry. It may be added in this connection that the village of Wheelock was, in 1873, a distinct parish, and that the living was accounted a vicarage, in the gift of the rector of Sandback. The population of the village then numbered 2,146.

It appears from Booth's "Pedigree and Dugdale's Visitation," 1663-4, that the "Arms of Wheelock" were of the following description: "*Argent, a chevron between three Catherine wheels Sable.*" (See cut in this book, which was taken from Ormerod's Cheshire.) "Burke's Encyclopædia of Heraldry" gives but one Wheelock coat-of-arms, and describes it precisely as above, placing the family in Wheelock county, Chester, the county that was formerly known as Cheshire. It may be of interest to know that the " Leversage of Wheelock" coat-of-arms is thus described in " The Visitation of Chester," 1580: — "*Arms — Quarterly — 1 and 4. Argent, a chevron between three ploughshares Sable. 2 and 3. Argent, a chevron between three Catherine wheels Sable. [Wheelock.] Crest.— a leopard's head jessant-de-lis Or.*" From this it would appear that, after the marriage of Agnes Whelock to Richard de Leversage, the Wheelock arms were incorporated with those of the Leversages. But, from the quotations made above, from Booth and Burke, it is evident that there were Wheelocks of later times, who were still entitled to the distinctive arms of the Wheelock family, as illustrated in our cut.

As no mention has been discovered of any other of the name of Ralph Wheelock as having emigrated to America from England, and three credible authorities declare that the one who settled in Dedham was he who was born in Shropshire County, England, we may therefore safely affirm that this man was indeed the ancestor of the Wheelock family in this country, which has now become a multitude in number and is widely scattered over the land. They may not reach "from Maine to Georgia," but certainly do reach from Vermont to Nebraska, and even to California, as the recent departure of Benjamin Ide Wheeler, a lineal descendant of Ralph Wheelock, to assume the presidency of the University of California, will clearly show. It may be added that a town of "Wheelock," in Vermont, is indexed in the United States Post-Office Directory, and that Nebraska also has a town of the same name. There are also descendants of Ralph Wheelock in North and South Dakota, Texas, New Mexico, and Colorado; Senator Edward O. Wolcott, of the latter state, being one of the number.

All of this vast multitude have sprung from Mr. Wheelock's nine children, whose names were as follows: Gershom, Mary, Benjamin, Samuel, Peregrine, Rebecca, Record, Experience, and Eleazer, most of whom, if not all, were married and raised large families; and their descendants of the early New England days multiplied rapidly, eight or ten children being the average allotment to each family,— an indication of the great vitality of the stock, of which we have further proof in the pronounced longevity to which, as the records show, many attained, even to fourscore and more years. The starting-point of this great multitude, after Dedham, Massachusetts, was in Medfield.

In Tilden's History of this town it is related that Ralph Wheelock's house-lot was the first granted in that town, and was at the corner of Main and North streets, the site lately owned by Elijah Thayer. There were twelve acres in his lot. His house, which was built in 1651–52, stood on the north side of Main street. From that historic spot the children went out to settle in Medfield, Mendon, Dedham, Uxbridge, Shrewsbury, Rehoboth, and adjoining regions, many of them becoming large land-owners and acquiring positions of prominence in the affairs of the towns. By reference to Ward's History of Shrewsbury, Tilden's History of Medfield, Ballou's History of Milford, and the records of the towns of Dedham, Grafton, Mendon, and Uxbridge, it will be found that many Wheelocks of character have appeared, who were prominent in the early days of New England, in town, State, and national affairs; and who, in council, good works, and exemplary lives, have left behind them a reputation and influence for good which ever continues.

Perhaps in nothing has the family been more prominent during these many generations than in its teaching capacity. Each succeeding generation has furnished many able teachers who have apparently inherited the gift or talent of Ralph Wheelock, and many of the present generation have chosen teaching for their vocation and life-work. Eleazer Wheelock, known in his day as "Master Wheelock," a grandson of Ralph, taught from 1756 to 1775, and lived on the original homestead, the house of which was not torn down until 1780. It was to a nephew of Master Whee-lock's wife, Simeon Plimpton by name, that the estate was given. Joseph Wheelock, a son of Ephraim, kept school in 1736, was a selectman from 1767 to 1774, and owned various lands. Perhaps the most prominent in the profession was Rev. Eleazer Wheelock, the first president of Dartmouth College, of whom it has been written: "His friends cherished the most cordial affection and profound veneration. He will be tenderly remembered while any are alive who ever knew him. His services will be gratefully recollected while civilization, science, and religion are dear to man." He is spoken of as one who, "by the gospel, subdued the ferocity of the savage, and to the civilized opened new pastures of science. He was a man of profound science and a fine classical scholar." His mantle seems to have fallen upon his son John, who succeeded him in the presidency of Dartmouth College.

But in other pursuits than the quiet one of the teacher did the early Wheelock ancestry also distinguish themselves. For courage and patriotism were they noted from the days of Gershom, the son of Ralph, who is said to have been " a mighty hunter of wild beasts," through the days of the Colonial Wars, to the end of the Revolutionary War.   Another son of Ralph, and grandfather of President Wheelock, Eleazer of Medfield, who afterwards removed to Mendon, is an illustration.   It is related "that he commanded a corps of cavalry, and was very successful in repelling the irruptions of the Indians upon the new settlements, and became extensively known and feared by those sons of violence and murder. He treated them with great kindness and humanity in peace, and, frequently joining them in the chase, he reconnoitered the country and discovered their retreats.   During the war with the Indians his house in Mendon was converted into a garrison, to which the settlers in the vicinity resorted for safety.   It was several times besieged, and in imminent danger, but providentially preserved."   Ephraim, a great-grandson of Ralph, served four years in the French and Indian Wars, and was a captain at the siege of Louisburg.   He was also a colonel in the War of the Revolution, and commanded a regiment in the Continental Army.   He was at Ticonderoga and Crown Point.   It is further related of him that he was in the first council of war of

7

the Revolution, held at Cambridge, April 20, 1775. Anthony Wheelock, who mustered a company into service at Worcester, Mass., in 1760, was a commissary. Captain Moses Wheelock, great-grandson of Ralph, born in 1737, died 1801, who was settled in Westboro, was in the regiment of Col. Artemus Ward. Captain Gershom Wheelock, of Shrewsbury, who is said to have been the first settler in that town, was one of the first appointed sergeants in a certain military company. He became an ensign, a lieutenant, and, in 1742, commanded as captain in the regiment of Col. Nahum Ward. He died in 1770, aged 77 years. Simeon Wheelock, another of Ralph's great-grandsons, of Uxbridge, Mass., was appointed one of a committee, by act of the town, to correspond with other committees with reference to the difficulty between Great Britain and North America. He, too, was in the Revolutionary War, and, at the call of Lexington, acted as first lieutenant in a company of Minute Men.

Later generations of the Wheelock family have generally applied their talents to manufacturing and mercantile pursuits, and have become successful and prominent in these lines. Not a few, however, have embraced the professions, and some have become missionaries, bearing the name with honor to themselves and to the family at large.

Perhaps enough has been written to prove that our ancestors were men of character and led lives worthy of emulation, and have left their descendants a heritage of no mean quality, but one in which we may surely take pride. If what has been shown shall incite those of this and following generations to keep the name of Wheelock inviolate from all evil, and inspire them with an ambition to prove themselves worthy successors of an ancient and honored name, then this little book will not have been prepared in vain.

THOMAS SEABURY WHEELOCK.

[NOTE.— Owing to the difficulty of reproducing the fine lines of the coat-of-arms in an impression on the outside of the book, the liberty has been taken, contrary to the announcement, to have a picture taken by a new process, and inserted as a separate leaf within the book. By this change of plan a much more faithful copy of the cut in Ormerod's Cheshire has been obtained than could have been secured by the first plan.]

www.ingramcontent.com/pod-product-compliance
Lightning Source LLC
Chambersburg PA
CBHW031815090426
42739CB00008B/1283